Understanding the Far-Left Psychosis
By George Koleszarik M.S.

Understanding the Far-Left Psychosis

EAN-13 9781441466631
ISBN 1441466630

This book is dedicated to my one and only son who has been my inspiration since before his birth in December, 1992

Acknowledgements

While writing this book has been fun and enjoyable for me, those around me may not have enjoyed my distant demeanor during the writing process. For this reason I wish to thank all those around me, including both family and friends for their patience and support while this project was being completed.

I would also like to express my appreciation to every writing teacher and professor I ever had that bothered to take an interest in my abilities. Armed with their red pens, these selfless educators helped to shape me into somewhat of a coherent writer despite my insolence.

Table of Contents

Preface

This book attacks the far-left in a sharp, biting, politically incorrect albeit humorous manner. This book will no doubt offend many who read it. If you are looking for a politically correct book please set this one down and just walk away. You have been warned. This book speaks the truth. If the readers of this book are offended by its contents, odds are good that they needed to be offended. The truth hurts and the truth shall set you free but sometimes it will first anger you beyond compare.

After many years of observing the steady decline of American values in this country and doing nothing about it, the worm has turned. If you are open minded and possess a highly developed sense of humor you will laugh out loud at the contents of this book. If you are an ultra-sensitive, politically correct, and narrow minded liberal you will be furious. If you are indeed driven to take action against the author of this book, please send a letter to someone who would be concerned and might actually respond to your whining.

Chapter 1
The Leftist Implications of the 2008 Election

As if we needed further proof that the United States is spiraling down the path of Socialism sprinkled with an ample helping of hedonism thrown in, witness the Republican nomination of John McCain for the President of the United States of America. The fact that John McCain was elected as the republican nominee is an ominous harbinger of the death of conservatism. Although the prospects for a third party's success are slim, true conservatives are no longer being justly represented by the Republican Party and may need to consider branching out on their own.

Despite the fact that John McCain has justly earned the respect and admiration of most Americans (including democrats) for his military service and selfless acts as a prisoner of war, he can scarcely be designated a conservative. When your three most famous accomplishments in the Senate are co-named Kennedy, Feingold, and Lieberman, it is not difficult to surmise that the word conservative is not featured prominently on your resume. Because there was previous speculation that McCain was being considered to be John Kerry's running mate in 2004 and because of more recent rumors that Lieberman could have been a potential vice presidential candidate in 2008, it is no wonder that conservatives were leery of McCain leading the government of the people.

The Republican Party had a chance to elect a true conservative in the guise of Fred Thompson yet at the time the Republican Party remained apathetic towards the grand Tennessean. Mister Thompson's lack of blind ambition was too foreign a concept to the illiterate pundits who could only surmise it connoted lethargy and apathy.

Consistency is vital to instilling trust and security to the American people. Ironically, consistency is what hampered Fred Thompson's campaign. While Romney, McCain, and Huckabee tailored their messages and resumes to suit the demographic du jour, Thompson remained true to himself, his record, and his conservative roots by never altering his message or resume. It is one thing to boast about straight talk and an entirely different thing to walk the straight walk. The time to wake up has passed for 2008 and it is too late to elect a President who cherishes, fights for, and adheres to the values and principles that true conservatives hold dear.

For a genuine conservative voter the 2008 Presidential election presented a dilemma. While it is a sheer disaster that a socialistic liberal democrat like Obama was elected President, a vote for McCain implied an acceptance, or at the very least, an admission that the Republican Party and the entire country has just taken a giant step left. An Obama win certainly shifted the drive to socialism into high gear just as a McCain win would have kept the United States on the steady path to becoming Canada.

Its not that McCain isn't sincere it's just that he is misguided. He truly loves America and fights doggedly for what he believes is best for the United States. McCain's problem is that shamnesty for twelve million criminals, raising taxes, and molly coddling terrorists does not make for a strong secure America and true conservatives should not sit quietly by and allow it to happen. Allowing 12 million criminals access to social services, public schools, and free health care is just another tug on the rope pulling us leftward. Although McCain says he intends to keep the tax cuts permanent, he previously would only do so under certain conditions. McCain has changed his mind on immigration and taxes due to public outcry. How can we know for sure that these new found positions are genuine or just political maneuvering?

As for Obama's policy of suckling terrorists, it is understandable that he has a deep aversion regarding torture but excuses for not using any means necessary to derive information from terrorists are flimsy. The fact that torturing terrorists does not provide valuable information is deeply disputed. Also, it is beyond fantasy to say that if we do not torture terrorists, then somehow they will see the light and treat their prisoners the way we treat ours. Besides, any student in your average 1960's parochial school suffered more abuse and humiliation than any Muslim terrorist has in Guantanamo Bay. It is impossible to fathom the degree of naivety which produces the belief that if we are nice to our Muslim terrorist captives, that somehow they will cease their decapitations, tortures, and plain old murders. Wake up! They hate us. They will never stop trying to kill us and they will never stop trying to inflict their morbid fanatical beliefs on all with whom they disagree

How many of our tax dollars have gone to keep the likes of Zacarias Moussaoui fat and happy? Why are we spending millions of dollars to feed, clothe, mother, and shelter these animals in Guantanamo Bay when a water board, a bullet, and an at sea burial can be had for a few dollars? The at sea burial should be especially appealing to our environmentally conscious friends as it will help to nurture the diminishing shark population and is non-pollutive providing the bullet is previously removed for recycling.

It is obvious that these malevolent Muslims have no remorse, no feeling, and no conscience. It is time we quit wasting tax dollars on these radical terrorists who are known murderers of innocent civilians. We may consider however to grant our tax dollars to be used for temporary housing, genital-sized jumper cables, and car batteries while these beasts are interrogated by whatever means necessary.

These liberal beliefs that everyone in the world deserves all the rights our constitution provides American citizens, whether they're citizens are not, only serves to weaken our security and therefore our nation. Thanks to the liberal leanings of leaders like McCain, not only is the United States seen as evil for slapping the terrorist's hands, foreign terrorists now have the right to a speedy trial.

The democrats' primary nominating process itself is further proof of our death slide into liberal fascism. Although our Founding Fathers' system of government allows everyone to say who represents them in government, the Electoral College process never quite sat right with some. This is because even though candidates can win the popular vote, they can still lose the election.

If a candidate obtains more delegates in the Electoral College by winning certain states, they can win the election with less popular votes. Still, since the Electoral College was set up by those wiser than us hundreds of year ago, we must accept it as our democratic process.

Let's examine the 2008 democratic primary elections. Not only can candidates in the Democratic Party win by state delegates and lose the popular vote, they can win without the majority of state delegates or the popular vote. In today's Democratic Party elections, an elite group of "super" delegates determines the outcome of elections. By totally disregarding the votes of the people, these "super" delegates can nominate whomever they chose.

Isn't having an elite group of "Super" people pick a Presidential candidate tantamount to fascism? The fact that eight hundred individuals can override the will of eighteen million is not democracy. No protest? No rebellion over this super delegate process? The fact that super delegates even exist demonstrates the fascist, socialistic philosophy inherent in the Democratic Party. God forbid they trust their own members. Oops, never mind, they don't believe in God.

Whether the "super" delegates determined the outcome of the election or not, the fact that they even have the power to determine the nominee means democracy has been abandoned.

When a candidate with no real experience, like Obama, is elected for President of the United States, it is a clear sign that liberals are enamored more by style than by substance. Democrats are so infatuated by Obama's smooth delivery they cannot bring themselves to see reality. Part of this reality being that Obama cut his political teeth in Chicago. Anyone who has spent any serious time in Chicago and its suburbs learns early on that the region's politics are wrought with corruption, greed, and cutthroat tactics. Needless to say, to rise to the top of such a rugged and dirty political environment, a Chicago politician needs to adapt to his or her surroundings. By consorting with the likes of Wright, Rezko, and Ayers (the ones vetted so far) Obama adapted and excelled in a town where the word politician is literally synonymous with crook. There is a reason why any good parent scrutinizes their child's friends. A person's character and beliefs can be discovered by the company he keeps. Didn't your Mother tell you that?

Can any liberal democrat actually believe that Obama sat in Reverend Wright's church for twenty years and did not subscribe to his venomous message of segregation? Since Obama's main campaign theme is change, let us hope that he intends to change his policy of oppressing the black community. It is ironic that Obama achieved his rise to power on the backs of the very people he claimed to champion all the while he was helping to hold them back. Obama is an oppressor of Blacks? How can this be?

By financially supporting reverend Wright's church, by subscribing to reverend Wright's vitriolic message for twenty years, and by enabling the status quo in the black community by providing entitlements, Obama is complicit in the oppression of the very community which he claims to champion.

Wright's message of anger, fear, and hatred of Whitey and America in general perpetuates bigotry and teaches the black community that they can never be successful in an integrated world. Instead of preaching togetherness, tolerance, and brotherly love among all people, Wright's philosophy of separatism and hatred ensures that his congregation remains dependent on government handouts, has limited hope, and has no vision beyond their own community.

This philosophy makes about as much sense as reparations. It was 160 years ago. Get over it and start making your own way. If we hold true to the spirit of reparations then enacting true justice would require putting every descendant of slaves back to their ancestors' original homelands. Any takers?

After twenty years of attendance in this divisive arena, it is impossible that Obama was unaware of the effects reverend Wright's acerbic message had on those around him. Like Jackson, Sharpton, and Wright before him, the Harvard educated Obama was keen enough to realize that dependent people are controllable people. If Wright's congregation were truly enlightened, then they would be self-reliant, responsible for their own problems, and have no need to blame the white man or government for their lot in life.

Obama is no leader. Obama is an oppressor. The true Black leaders are Michael Steele, Angela McGlowan, Larry elders, and even Bill Cosby. Because Michael, Angela, Larry, and Bill did not spend their days resenting the white man or the government, they spent their time bettering themselves, working hard, and maintaining a positive attitude thus enabling them all to rise to the top of their chosen fields. They did not listen to the prejudiced ravings of angry black leaders, but chose instead to cling to hope, hard work, and conservative values.

One can only hope that the followers of this Jacksonian and Sharptonesque dogma can open their eyes and minds to realize that the only thing holding them back is their own perceptions. Shame on you, Obama, for using your own church and community to further your own ambitions while stifling the hopes and dreams of those you purport to serve.

Emerson said "What you are shouts so loudly I cannot hear what you say". The problem is that half of Americans believe the rhetoric they hear and ignore the actions, record, and associations of the, would be messiah, who ascended from the sewer that is Chicago politics. After wallowing in the sludge for so many years, the smell does not wash away so easily.

With any luck, the blind that are fooled by the rhetoric and ignore the actions and associations of the man, will somehow awaken to the truth. It is becoming more and more evident that Obama is just another crooked Chicago style politician who does and says what ever he needs to misdirect his adoring public from the truth. Associations and friendships do matter. If the press had worked as hard to vet Obama as they did to prop him up early on, Hillary would have been the 2008 Presidential nominee. In this election, like anything else, we cannot count on the mainstream media to provide us with an accurate depiction either candidate. We will deal more with the left –wing media in another chapter.

If a republican candidate like McCain had won the election, it would have signaled the end of conservatism in the Republican Party and marked a dramatic shift left by a party that claims to be on the right. Since Obama won the election, then a socialist government in the United States is closer than ever.

Taxing big business, universal health care, and record new entitlements will help to stifle and eventually kill America's leadership in the world. It is difficult to comprehend how taking forty-five per cent of the job creators' money will be good for the economy. How Obama can view big business as evil, redistribute all of its profits, and regulate it to the point of being ineffectual and still claim he will create jobs for all - remains a mystery.

Perhaps it is a genetic deficiency or maybe some form of group hypnosis but for some reason liberals cannot fathom that competition (capitalism) leads to innovation and thus progress. As it stands now, the United States has the best health care system and medical research facilities in the world. By mandating insurance policy regulations, forcing doctors and pharmaceutical companies to give away their goods and services to everyone regardless of citizenship, universal health care would make great gains in destroying competition in our health care and research industries. Universal healthcare will also destroy our worldwide medical superiority in the process. When is the last time someone you knew who was seriously sick that said "I need the best health care I can find I'm going to Russia?"

While it is true there are many unfortunate people in the United States who need entitlements, there are undoubtedly more wasting away on their couches because they feel entitled. People who can work need to go to work. Liberals love to whine about high unemployment (even when it's low) while their democratic base of malingerers is home all day everyday watching the Jerry Springer Show. Why should the responsible hard working people's tax dollars go to finance someone who refuses to go to work, has six kids with six different fathers, and never learned to keep her legs shut? Many liberals actually find it sensible that we pay the way for those who believe that consuming crack cocaine is somehow a higher vocation. Our tax dollars were never meant to subsidize people's hedonistic, dysfunctional lifestyles.

America did not become the leader of the free world by embracing socialistic ideology. America became a super power by embracing competition in the market place, by working harder than everyone else, and by fostering opportunity. Liberals must learn that not everyone gets to win. Those with the best ideas, products, and performance get to be first and hence get to reap the rewards. Sorry little Brad and Chad but not everyone gets a trophy. Being born anywhere, let alone the United States does not entitle anybody to be number one in any arena. Until recently the American way has been hard work, family values, and a spirit of pride in competition. If you prefer to be equal in class with everyone else, prefer a thirty hour work week, and need government mandated nap times during your work day, it is strongly suggested you move to Europe.

Now it turns out that Obama is embarrassed of Americans because we do not speak French and he believes that our children must learn Spanish. Despite conservatives' abject sympathy for Obama's embarrassment at the United States' lack of foreign language prowess, conservatives do not share his emotion. Similarly, conservatives do not feel compelled to learn Spanish because some rookie politician says they must.

Since Obama was so worried about people thinking that visiting our wounded soldiers in Germany would be viewed as a political tactic, he chose not to go. Therefore, it is fair to say that Obama is more worried about public perception than doing what is right. Talk about courage.

If you voted against funding those who were severely wounded protecting my safety and you had no concern for the success of their mission, you, like Obama, would not be able to look them in the eye and would refuse to visit. The good news is there just may be a hint of conscience and shame in our would-be messiah.

Contrary to all the liberal posturing, a person cannot support the troops while not supporting their mission. That's like saying "I love construction workers and contractors but I wish there were no houses and buildings." Our troops are smarter than that and deserve better.

Conservatives do not aspire to be French, German, Spanish or any other European designation and we will not live our lives with the sole pursuit of pleasing foreign nations. Nor will should we ever be embarrassed of our country because some elitist seeking cocktail credibility blushes at the thought of being disliked by Cannes Film Festival regulars. We are Americans. We speak English. Sorry Barraq but America did not become a super power by emulating France. Can you name the last great invention that did not come out of the United States or Japan? Instead of being embarrassed that Americans are linguistically challenged abroad, show some pride that the entire world has learned English in order to do business with the United States.

Although conservatives do not agree with John

McCain on every issue, we whole heartedly believe he is a man of great character and integrity and towers over Obama in the areas of trustworthiness, judgment and experience. While McCain presents the persona of an elder statesman and hero, Obama comes off as a spoiled mendacious child conniving, hiding, and avoiding the facts to get his way.

Whenever controversy arises for the Obama campaign, they call it a distraction and say "we need to move on". Well, yes of course Obama needs to move on before the curtain is lifted and the wizard's true colors become evident.

If Obama can be mentored and preached to by a man for twenty years and not share, or at the very least know, the man's malodorous opinions and feelings about our great country, can we believe the man is telling the truth? If he is telling the truth can we trust his judgment? The sad truth is that McCain is not even close to being a true conservative and yet he is the best choice the Republican Party could come up with in 2008 to defeat Obama, lead our nation, and protect our values.

Chapter 2
Los Estados Unidos de Mexico

Bienvenidos! Welcome to the United States of Mexico. Sound far fetched? Think again. At the current rate of growth Spanish will become the dominant language in the United States. The United States Census Bureau claims there are twelve million illegal aliens currently in the United States. Really? Can they be certain? By their very nature illegal aliens are secretive, or as the liberal media would spin it, forced to live in the shadows. Assuredly, illegal aliens are not grabbing their friends and relatives by the hand and lining up to greet the census takers. The point is that the Census Bureau cannot be certain of how many people are here illegally. What is known for sure is that there are entire communities in the United States where English is not even spoken.

Illegal aliens come here not because they love the United States and wish to assimilate our ways and culture, but they come here to grab a few squares of roadway off of our paved with gold streets. By living together with several families all together in a small apartment, they can sustain themselves with virtually no bills. All the while they are making low wages and escaping taxes by getting paid under the table, they still manage to get healthcare, driving privileges, and free education. All this enables them to send the bulk of their earnings back to Mexico or whatever third world country from which they snuck over the border. For sacrificing in squalid, crowded, cramped conditions for many years, they are able to return home to two houses, nice cars, and even servants.

We cannot in good conscience exempt the landlords who rent to illegal aliens from punishment. These criminal abetting land owners not only provide illegals with a hiding place, they manage to bring down the property values of those law biding conscientious home owners who have the distinctive misfortune to live on a street with a duplex which doubles as the residential equivalent of a clown car.

We cannot blame the illegal aliens for wanting to come here and earn a better life for themselves and their families but we can blame the government for not securing the border and we can blame the businesses and landlords that provide them with opportunities and safe haven. The same can be said for every homeowner who hires an illegal unlicensed housekeeper, landscaper, or contractor. Shame on you and do not even think about complaining about your taxes when the people working for you are spared that irrelevant remittance to Uncle Sam.

Lest we forget the one world open borders crowd who feels that anyone anywhere has the right to come to our sovereign nation and be taken care of even if they are sporting gang tats and a ten page criminal record. To the open borders lobby it does not matter if illegals are criminals. Just because an illegal alien maims, kills, or rapes an American citizen is no reason they should suffer the gross indignation of being asked for their paperwork. How dare we impose such Orwellian measures like asking felons where they are from or if they have any identification? Oh, the humanity! These poor "immigrants" could be scarred for life and have nightmares of the day they were actually caught breaking the law.

Though seldom talked about in the media, there are those who come to this country not because they want to make a living but because they feel we stole this land from them in the Mexican American War. Que Lastima! Consider yourselves lucky we did not continue southward and just take the whole thing. These United States are wholly comprised of sections that were won in wars from England, Spain, France, and the Native Americans etc. Whether anyone likes it or not, this land is our land and we are never going to give it back. Or are we? A closer inspection reveals that Mexicans are indeed taking back the lands they lost in the Mexican war. Through unobstructed borders, rampant procreation, sanctuary cities, greedy businessmen, selfish landlords, and spineless politicians on both sides of the aisle, Mexico has already reclaimed entire sections of the United States.

There are now many areas and even entire towns in the United States where English is never spoken. The American government and businesses make it unnecessary for Spanish speakers to learn English. By providing all government and school documents in Spanish, by providing Spanish television and radio stations, and by businesses hiring people who do not speak English, an immigrant (legal or not) can live a comfortable informed life in the United States without ever having to speak, read, or write the English language.

There was a time when America was a beacon to the world. People of all nationalities dreamt of coming to America and toiled and sacrificed to make it happen. Not only were they coming for opportunity, they were coming because they loved the thought of America. They loved the entrepreneurial spirit, the freedom, and the strength of resolve America displayed to the rest of the world. In the past immigrants worked hard to learn English, learn the culture, and become part of our society. They waited ten long years at the chance to finally become an American Citizen and danced down the streets, their faces brimming over with pride after receiving the immense satisfaction that came with taking their vow of citizenship.

Diversity is a wonderful thing and is a big part of what makes America so special. In the past, we had diversity coupled with patriotism and a strong desire to belong. Now we just have diversity. Today's immigrants expect to have every single idiosyncrasy of their culture accommodated. Instead of maintaining their homeland's culture and traditions while aspiring to be part of a great America, every ethnic group and nationality expects to be put first.

Let's fast forward to the state of today's immigration. Not only do today's immigrants not bother to come here legally or learn our language, they have the audacity to rally and protest for rights to which they have no claim, all the while displaying the Mexican flag. Since fishermen are no longer able to use their huge nets to make a living, perhaps we can utilize the nets at the next illegal alien demonstration. How a person can illegally break into another country and demand goods, services, and the protection of that country's constitution is not only baffling it is the epitome of arrogance. It is like a burglar robbing an art gallery and asking to get their parking validated on the way out.

There are still some immigrant groups like the Cubans who truly appreciate America and what it has to offer. Because they live in a communistic oppressive regime, the Cuban people understand what a blessing it is to have basic unalienable rights. Why we never went down there and freed them is another mystery. They risk their lives in dramatic fashion to get here and are genuinely grateful when they arrive. They do not just wade across a river and demand welfare for their eight babies.

If you love and appreciate our country come on in we want you here. If you are here because you feel entitled to be here or you feel that we owe you something, you are not welcome. If an illegal immigrant says they love our country, we should give them a chance to prove it by serving four years in our military. If they survive and serve four years with honor, then they deserve to be on the fast track to naturalization.

Even if we wanted to, the United States does not have the space or the resources to accommodate the entire world. Just as we the people reserve the right to say who is allowed in our houses or places of business, the United States reserves the right to say who we allow in our country. Proximity does not denote worthiness or eligibility. If your neighbor's house costs fifteen million dollars and yours only costs one hundred thousand, you are not allowed to go stay in your neighbor's house merely because you are dissatisfied with your own position. In fact, if you attempted to cross the border into your neighbor's house, you could be legally shot and killed.

There is a reason why people live in gated communities and gated estates. They have a lot to lose and there are people out there who are willing to take it. If people didn't steal, there would be no need for security. To some, it is easier to steal what others have built and grown instead of building and growing their own. If people worked as hard building up their own countries as they work trying to break into ours, their countries' economies would be in much better shape and they would not feel the need to leave their own soil.

So, why then is our government unwilling or unable to provide our country with security? You guessed it – Hedonism. It would seem that it is more important to our politicians to get elected then to protect our treasure and way of life. As long as the politicians are in their seats of power enjoying their jet setter's lifestyle, it does not matter that our border is porous, our social security is waning, or that our very language is in danger of extinction. Since the United States is a super power, it is reasonable to deduct that we have the resources and know how to secure our own border. If we stopped furnishing free health care to twelve million illegal aliens, the socialist dream of universal health care would soon be obsolete. Similarly, if we got rid of every illegal alien with three or more social security numbers and the benefits that go with them, our social security system would be in much better shape.

Numerous times in the past our government has enacted laws which dealt severe fines and even jail time to businesses and landlords who hire and rent to illegal aliens. These laws and high profile cases oddly enough seem to cluster around election time. While these new laws and penalties make great headlines for awhile, they inevitably fade into obscurity until the next time the debate arises (the next election). These headlines are great for politicians trying to please their base but they must be careful not to anger their Hispanic constituents. So with a nod and a wink they let their Hispanic voters know that illegal immigration crack down is just temporary and America will soon forget about them again between elections. Although tragic to the American people, it will be humorous to watch the politicians vehemently remind us how they fought steadfastly to secure our countries borders after the next terrorist attack emanates from the Mexican border. Most Americans will hopefully realize these gutless politicians have been aware of the border problem for decades and yet the closest they ever got to solving it was sitting on their thumbs.

It is ironic that the self-proclaimed world's only super power can be so internally weak. Despite the fact that we have federal laws and procedures for dealing with illegal immigrants, we have mayors who decline to follow them without fear of punishment. When did it happen that big city mayors became exempt from the law? By ordering their police forces not to follow the law, these renegade mayors are engaged in conspiracy and are guilty of a felony themselves and should be punished accordingly. Since these mayors are probably citizens, they cannot legally be deported. However, if we decide to bring back the age old practice of exile, the United States does still hold some island territories which could prove useful for rehabilitating these socialist miscreants. Seriously, these mayors need to be brought to task by higher authorities. If every average citizen chose to pick and choose which laws were to be followed, the socialists would end up with anarchy instead of their androgynous, classless, raceless[sic], and godless utopia.

Instead of providing water stations to aid and abet these law breakers, why not deploy land mines and electric fences to help dissuade them from committing an infraction. As a punishment for their blatant allowance and education on how to cross our border, the pamphlet distributing Mexican government officials can be rounded up to build the electric fence and bury the mines. If this is too indignant a task for men of such credentials, perhaps we can offer them a dollar more over minimum wage and Obama could give them a payroll tax break. Or perhaps we can disguise these Mexican officials as Guatemalans in Guatemala and force them to try to sneak into Mexico. News flash, odds are they would be shot.

Still, in all good conscience our government insists on rewarding border criminals in numerous ways. Not only are border criminals rewarded with the before mentioned social services, health care, and education, if they have a baby on American soil, they get to be United States citizens. Would it make sense to use this reward system for any other crimes? If we follow our all knowing government's logic, then the daughter of a successful jewelry store robber should receive a diamond tiara and a new tennis bracelet every year for life courtesy of Uncle Sam and your average car thief should receive free gas and oil changes for life.

Some will argue that most Hispanics illegals are decent hard working Christian people that do not hurt anyone but only help contribute to our gross national product. How much higher would our GDP be if the billions and billions of untaxed dollars sent back over our borders were actually factored into the bottom line? While it is true that most illegal aliens are hard working etc, every single one of them broke the law when they crossed our border and should not be rewarded.

One question the illegal aliens and open border tofu lovers may want to ask themselves is - where will all the illegal aliens seek their refuge and fortunes after they have turned the United States into a third world nation with no opportunities. America's descent into a third world country is a scenario which, by the way, has already begun and is well under way.

Chapter 3
Why Liberals Hate God

Any psychologist worth his hypnosis inducing timepiece will tell you that hate is born out of anger and anger emanates from fear. So why do liberals fear God so much? The answer is simple, if there is a God, then living the liberal hedonistic philosophy of immorality, perversion, and me-first attitude will have no consequences in the afterlife. If there is no God then liberals may do as they like without the inconvenient pangs of conscience, guilt, and shame as well as no fear of eternal retribution. As far as earthly consequences go for their unabashed hedonism, these patented pagans need only move to Vermont, Las Vegas, or San Francisco to avoid castigation.

Now many liberals will dispute the fact that they hate God claiming that they even go to church. While it may be true that many liberals have some sort of weak relationship with a higher power, they certainly do not love God. If you love something or someone, you want them with you always, you want to see them wherever you go, you do not try to block them from your eyes, ears, and every square inch of public domain.

How disturbing it must be to our liberal brethren when they go to visit their back-alley abortionist, their Las Vegas hookers, or their nearest street corner medical marijuana pharmacist and have to pay with United States currency proudly displaying the words "In God We Trust." Deep down these masters of self-denial know that constantly relenting to their basest instincts is wrong which is indeed why they need to erase all mentions of God and Christianity from public domain. Having God visible in court rooms, schools, our pledge of allegiance, or even on our money is a stark reminder to these hedonists that maybe just maybe, the selfish devoid of values life they are leading is not the life the human race was meant to live.

Queasy readers may wish to skip this next paragraph. Unless there is no God, how on earth could any compassionate human being snuff out the life of a fully formed baby by crushing its tiny head two weeks before it is born? This vile, disgusting act of late-term abortion is the ultimate act of selfishness. Some may argue that suicide is the ultimate act of selfishness but an ACLU NAMBLA loving, late term abortion wanting, God hating liberal's suicide may just be seen by God as an act of justice, compassion and the only logical course of action.

Speaking of the National Man Boy Love Association, could any liberal with any hint of brains think that raping our children is a perfectly acceptable pursuit unless there is no God. It is amazing that any liberals whatsoever even have children. A liberal with children must be considered scientific proof of mental deficiency. How could any parent promote the virtues of an organization like the American Civil Liberties Union which promotes NAMBLA, the erasure of God from all society, and the release of criminals and terrorists from all prisons and still be charged with shaping the fragile minds of our nation's greatest resource?

Yes, living a life with no God or even a hint of God has many advantages. Having no God makes promiscuity, drug use, alcoholism, infanticide, child molestation, and malingering all perfectly reasonable. While having no God makes it ok to harm our children, don't you dare bring harm to the rocky mountain spotted burrowing whooping moth. Another travesty of justice built into this Godless group is that the true great Americans, the ones that work hard, raise children, worship God, defend our country, and pay their taxes are the very ones who our supporting these simpleton morons who believe that lack of God allows them to wallow in decadence at our expense.

Despite the facts that George Washington, the Father of our country, refused to be inaugurated President without a bible to swear on, ninety per cent of Americans believe in God in some form or another, and the main theme of all major religions is helping your neighbor, these liberal idiots still argue that God should have no part in our Government, schools or public lives. Democracy or majority rules have no meaning to the hedonistic. Democracy to them means that they should get whatever they want, whenever they want, however they want and the government needs to make it happen for them or they'll call their lawyers in the ACLU.

Thanks to our hedonistic liberal chums, The Ten Commandments, a perfectly healthy and wise guide for good living, are no longer allowed to be displayed in our Nation's court houses. Heaven help a criminal who walks into a court room and catches a glimpse of the Ten Commandments. Are the atheist liberals afraid that Johnny Rapist may find Jesus before he gets to prison? Not only are the Ten Commandments are no longer present in the court room the Godless have even managed to remove another long standing Christian tradition in the court room – swearing on the Bible. When these poor atheists were called to testify, they had to raise one hand and place the other on the Bible thus hindering any attempt to cross their fingers behind their backs which would, no doubt, in their minds legally negate the oath to God.

One favorite argument of our deity challenged cohabitants is to point out the hypocrisy of the conservative right whenever one of our members has a fall from grace. It is true that conservatives are not perfect and do occasionally engage in debauchery and less than reputable behavior. The difference is that conservatives have a moral vision and ideals. Conservatives desire and work towards a world with values, morals, self-sacrifice, and altruism. Though we conservatives are human beings and do fall short of these ideals from time to time, we are nonetheless striving to achieve them in our everyday lives and know in our hearts that faith in God, country, and family values are the keys to success.

The liberal lordless [sic] however, do not know the meaning of the words altruism or self-sacrifice.

Since we explained the conservative vision and ideals, it is only fair we illuminate the atheists' vision and ideals. Philanthropy to our leftist friends can only mean donating money to any cause whose sole mission is to squash any organization that has conservative leanings. Even though liberals despise our founding fathers, they need to remember they have the right to pursue happiness, not have happiness handed to them by the very government they disdain. What an impossible quandary encumbers the pea-sized brains of the entitled. Because the entitled need the welfare that the God-fearing federal government so graciously allows them, they cannot outright destroy their bureaucratic benefactor but must instead work to evolve it over time into a true socialist enterprise. What these heathens fail to realize is that once the United States is ruled by a Socialist government, we will no longer have the resources to fund their daily excursions into the realms of evil.

Family values are part of the liberal's vision but in their version any discussion of family values is only acceptable providing the parents raising the children are named Frank and Eric. Another suitable scenario for a liberal family consists of a single lesbian mother who was artificially inseminated from the DNA taken from either Tim Robbins or Susan Sarandon. Adhering to traditional family values requires hard work, self sacrifice, and a basic sense of right and wrong. Since these are all foreign concepts to those that would destroy the moral fabric of America, it is no wonder that the traditional family frightens them as much as the thought of there being a God.

The Christ haters need so badly to stay in denial that they have a Linda Bair-like reaction at the thought of a child reciting the word God every morning before the start of school. Since they hate God, and our county is built on God's principles, it stands to reason that they would also hate their own country. How ironic that the majority of the people who have fought and died to protect and retain the freedoms that ensure that these lowlifes are able to pursue their abhorrent activities, are Christians. Liberals have yet to produce a coherent explanation of why they find it acceptable for Muslim children to pray to Mecca five times a day in public schools and wash their feet in public school bathrooms while in the very same schools it is not acceptable for

Christian children to recite the pledge of allegiance because it contains the word God or even discuss the possibility of creationism. The power of Christ compels you! The power of Christ compels you!

The ACLU and their fanatic cronies are every bit as zealous trying to obliterate God from society as Tomas de Torquemada was in trying to purify the people of Europe during the Spanish Inquisition. How defiled and bitter must a person's psyche be to drive them to boil over at the sight of a baby in a manger, a Christmas tree, or even a menorah? What level of deranged psychosis leads a human being to think of a child saying grace aloud in a public school lunchroom as a cause for litigation? Do the psycho liberals really spend so much time and effort to keep their children away from the thought of God that any reference to God suffered by their child is perceived as mental contamination and thus grounds for a lawsuit? Don't worry Mr. Psycho Liberal, someday little Jenny will attend Berkley where she will have every memory of anything to do with God methodically removed by the liberal arts professor with whom she is currently sleeping.

Biblical sayings like "love they neighbor as thyself" and "give and ye shall receive" are atheistic blasphemy. How hearing such enlightened and beautiful concepts can cause someone a panic attack remains unclear. Perhaps the atheists in question are aware they have already exhausted their own futile attempts at redemption and have just given up on being human. Regardless, they are by far the minority in this and every other country on earth and should not be given their way just to appease some ACLU high priced lawyers and the press.

Chapter 4
The Left Stream Media

Although it may seem that some of the topics in this book are obvious and should go without saying, there are still many who are unaware or are unwilling to see how the far left is systematically destroying the wholesome way of life which has made America great. A major force in the systematic destruction of American values and security is the mainstream media. To that end we will continue to pummel the proverbial equine corpse until those with the ability to reason stand up and boycott the liberal press establishments who feel no obligation to report the facts.

Ah, what to say about the New York Times. It may be worth noting that if the New York Times behaved in the year 1944 like it does today, the publisher and managing editor could have been hung for treason or at the very least imprisoned for sedition. Unfathomable is the only word to describe a news outlet that would publicize top-secret programs of the government just to curry political favor for their party, sell newspapers, and embarrass the party currently in power with whom they happen to disagree. Even more incredulous is that even though the government specifically asked the Times not to print the story because it would endanger American lives and put an end to a program that was vital to United States security, they printed the stories anyway. Not only did the so called paper of record defy their government and expose top-secret programs, they did so without any punishment or reprisal of any kind. The cowardly traitors are too ignorant and callous to even suffer a hint of remorse, guilt, or shame for their subversive actions.

So long as the Times and its clone-like flower power graduate run newspapers continue to promote the far-left's agenda, books, movies, and candidates, they will continue to amass an audience of sheep-parrot hybrids to regurgitate their socialist hedonistic philosophy. The leftist media's strength draws from ubiquity and repetition. If enough people hear an untruth enough times from enough places, they start to believe it.

The New York Times is not content with disrupting secret operations, spewing left wing dogma, and trying to control what everyone watches and reads, they will not be satisfied until they help the United States lose a war. So hungry is the Slime's need to help us lose in Iraq, they have gone so far as to print stories that are one hundred per cent imagined, print only the negative news from Iraq, and do their best ignore the progress which has without a doubt been made by the surge.

Oddly enough, there are still many conservatives who can be spotted reading the infamous bird cage liner. Would you believe there is scientific data documenting parakeets, macaws, and African grays refusing to go on the *New York Times* in their cages? The birds were quoted as saying that "the paper was unworthy of receiving their excrement." Admittedly, the Times does have a good crossword puzzle but beyond that it is hard to understand why any right minded conservative would give fifty cents a day to one of America's worst enemies especially when there are now alternatives on the market like the *New York Post* and the *Wall Street Journal*.

If we begin to dissect the intent and philosophies of the weekly news magazines, we find that they have evolved from the same branch of the family tree as the

New York Times. It is safe to say that *Newsweek* and *Time Magazine* are the "*New York Times* Lite" without the coupons, advertisers, or the readers. Since the number of advertisers for these rancorous rags is in short supply and shrinking every year, it is difficult to comprehend how these myopic print houses stay in business. Luckily, that liberal philanthropy we discussed earlier is alive and well and for now able to keep these lefty lopsided institutions afloat.

The longer one listens and subscribes to these main stream media outlets, the more he becomes convinced that conservatives are Caesar reincarnate. If America is and always has been hell bent on world domination, why do we not currently own Japan and Germany? Surely we could invade and conquer Mexico and Canada at our leisure some sunny Sunday afternoon and then lazily make our way down through South America over the summer.

The reason liberals cannot see that America is a force for good and freedom in the world that sacrifices more blood and money than all other nations combined for the preservation and expansion of freedom, is that it is an altruistic ideal. The thought of a person, let alone a nation, sacrificing their lives and treasure towards a noble end without compensation is so mind-boggling to the hedonist liberals that they are incapable of believing that it's true. Liberals therefore need to manufacture and assign cynical motives so they can make sense of our selfless actions abroad.

Unfortunately for the liberal mass media, their message that conservative Americans are all bible thumping imperialists intent on ruling the world does not sell well enough to compete in the market place. One place this lack of skill at left-wing message dissemination is blatantly obvious is on the radio. So poorly developed are the liberals talk radio entertainment skills that they nearly bankrupted National Public Radio. After all, how many hours can a person spend listening to the cynical bitter ravings of emotionally sterile men and women devoid of humor and with no prospects who were picked last for every gym class activity in high school? So mortified were these no talent hacks of the utter radio failure, they ran whining to the liberal congress like the spoiled brat on the playground that never got his turn on the see-saw.

No big shock then that the democratic lead congress actually tried to pass a law that would mandate equal air time for both liberal and conservative pundits.

Forget socialism, we are now entering the realms of communism and fascism. This is still America? We are still a capitalist country? We are so sorry Mz. Pelozi and wannabe senator Mister Franken, but the free market is what set the prices and schedules for radio shows. The more people listening to a show, the more money advertisers pay. Perhaps our liberal congress could create a new research grant that can figure out how to teach left-wingers to laugh and at least appear aurally to have the rudiments of a personality. Speaking of Pelozi, watching her give a speech conjures up image of a Westworld reject that somehow managed.

Enter Rush Limbaugh and FOX News. What a pleasure it would have been to be in the National Public Radio executive board room to see the faces of those failures when the announcement of Rush Limbaugh's four hundred million dollar contract was made. No doubt antacid sales have quadrupled since the announcement. The far left cannot conceive that Rush earned this money by attracting extraordinary numbers of listeners and advertisers, it must be a ploy by the vast right wing conspiracy to abolish liberal radio once and for all. After all conservatives are synonymous with big business and they could all easily chip in to bring this major propaganda coup to fruition. Sorry Stuart Smalley but the truth is Mister Limbaugh earned every penny.

Similarly the liberals detest FOX News because they have been winning the market share for the last eight years. Liberals whine that Fox News is not true to its "fair and balanced" slogan but leans heavily to the right. Since Fox gave Laura Ingraham her own slot, there is no point arguing that they do not lean right. Well of course FOX leans to the right and thank God it does. Without Rush and FOX the liberal media would have the only voice informing the American people and the world what is really happening. While FOX News does slant towards the right, it still manages to be more fair and balanced than any of the other network, radio, or cable news shows. How ironic that the top spokesman for the Hillary Clinton primary campaign praised FOX as being the fairest cable news channel. When Hillary is not leftist enough for half the country, you know we are spiraling out of control. The truth is that even though FOX has a conservative preference, they make a point of providing both conservative and liberal viewpoints for every issue.

Also, very telling is that although the O'Reilly Factor is the most popular cable news show on television by far, Obama refused to go on for nearly two tears. Obama is a man who does not have the time to go on the O'Reilly Factor, the most watched cable news show in the country, yet he seems to always have ample time to pencil in Ellen, The View, American Idol, Saturday Night Live, and Jon Stewart to name just a few. He calls himself a Uniter [sic] but has consistently excluded millions of potential voters and tough questions by hiding out in friendly liberal venues.

So hated is FOX News by its left coast arch enemies that if a democratic candidate even appears on the FOX News network, that candidate is promptly excoriated and ridiculed on every left leaning blog on the internet. It is amazing that such malice can exist in the minds of people for a news network especially when these tree hugging sprout eaters have never even bothered to watch any of the network's shows.

Chapter 5
Las Vegas and Hollyweird

At least the ancient Egyptians' defining achievement, the pyramids, had the noble aim of sheltering a king's body and soul until the soul could make its final transition to the heavens. It will be a sad day when future archeologists look back on today's civilization and realize that our greatest accomplishment out west was a glass and steel pyramid whose only function was to shelter inhabitants while they engaged in games of greed and chance.

Las Vegas is one of the few places in America that comes close to the hedonist liberals' ideal society. The city's advertising campaign plays like a liberal's wet dream. Come to Las Vegas and cheat on your spouse! Need hookers? No problem. Lose your 401k and kid's college fund? We can help that's why we're here. What happens in Vegas stays in Vegas, except maybe the venereal diseases you bring home to your loved ones.

Falling under the category of sad but true, America's most famous desert city proudly boasts of its immorality and uses its easy debauchery access as its major selling point for tourism in its television commercials with great pride.

Notwithstanding the gambling, legalized prostitution, and omnipresent opportunities for infidelity, liberals won't quite be happy until Las Vegas combines its own neurosis with the drug policies of Amsterdam, the marriage laws of Taxassachusetts, and the all out insanity of San Francisco. To a liberal hedonist, there is no concept of sin let alone a concept of moderation and decency. Forget the "me generation" we now have an entire me movement working diligently to turn the United States into Sodom and Gomorrah. It is difficult to discern if Hollyweird is Sodom and Las Vegas is Gomorrah or visa versa. Either way they both have earned their respective titles.

Hollywood, here is a bit of wisdom for you. You cannot support the troops and abhor their mission at the same time. You cannot on one hand say we love and respect you and on the other hand say even though you believe whole heartedly in what you're doing, we think what you're doing is evil and want it stopped. That's like saying we love the construction workers but we disapprove of buildings and houses. How many times have we heard that old gem "Our troops are in danger" or "Our troops are in harm's way?" Here is another news flash for our Chinese theater adornments and their liberal media cohorts that's what troops do; they fight, go into danger, and yes go into harm's way. That is their purpose. That is what they're trained to do. What would these sage stars of screen have our soldiers do, pass out milk and cookies to the illegal aliens as they stream across the border?

In fact, our troops go into harm's way so the likes of Danny Glover and Sean Penn have the right to sit up on their stages and wax philosophical on how the world would be a better place if we all thought like Hugo Chaves. What is it in the Hollyweird hills water source that makes one wake up one day and think – It would be really cool to hang out with a dictator. After the ceremonial mass consumption of magic mushrooms during the trip to their tyrant of choice's palace, these testicle-free entertainment legends have no other recourse but to come back to the United States and announce the revelation that it's the United States' fault that rulers like Castro are cranky. People like Harry

Belafonte don't care that the people in these wretched regimes are oppressed though violence, imprisoned for speaking their demands, or denied access to the outside world so long as their leader provides some really good cigars and wants them to produce a movie.

How ashamed and emasculated the Hollyweird posers of today must feel compared to their heroic predecessors. The truly admirable ones were heroes like Jimmy Stewart who gave up a lucrative career in Hollywood movies to go and risk his life serving his country. Such unbelievable selflessness was displayed by countless big name stars in the old Hollywood days when men were men and didn't whine that they were to pretty to go and fight without makeup. The best Hollywood's brightest can manage today is a pathetic protest rally lead by their hero and mentor Hanoi Jane belting out their mantra "we support the troops but…." Let us not forget our sultry inebriated starlets' role in all of this patriotic dissent. In the 1940's women were not concerning themselves with their boob size, latest Louis Vutton creation, or most recent diet. The women of the 1940's were joining the Red Cross, producing munitions in factories, raising money for the cause, and intentionally going without in order to unselfishly assist their country - that my half-plastic botulism-encrusted icons is patriotism.

These Hollywood heroes cannot see past their hatred for President Bush and are therefore blinded to the amazing benefits that would derive from a free Iraq. The left-coast liberals cannot see that a free Iraq would bring us another strong ally in the Middle East, bring us another productive competitor in the world market, and give the Iraqi people the freedom and opportunities they deserve. A free and democratic Iraq would provide a major force of stabilization in a region ruled by chaos. The Hollyweirdos care not for the people of Iraq or for the Middle East, they care only that President Bush is disgraced and humiliated. This unreasonable hatred is so strong that they would sacrifice the security of our country and other countries to ensure that the commander in chief that they loathe does not succeed. It is ironic that although President Bush is doing his best to preserve and secure the greatest free land on the planet, the very people he does his utmost to protect are capable of nothing but spite and degradation in return.

Let us take a closer look at the Hollywood pansies' unyielding broken argument that this war against terror is nothing like fighting the Japanese and Nazis in World

War II. Oh really? Let's see now. Three thousand innocent civilians were senselessly murdered, they tried to sink one of our war ships, there is a methodical systematic ongoing effort to destroy the western way of life and root out and stifle any semblance of other cultures, the fanatical Muslims kill everyone who does not agree with their creed, and they are conditioning their youth to hate certain races, yet all this doesn't seem familiar to anyone out there in tinsel town? Not ringing any bells yet? Anyone? Bueller?

I guess it is easier to play ostrich and make movies agreeing with the terrorists' position than actually having to go and fight. These left wing cinematic expressions of disgust for their own country, otherwise known as movies, serve only to embolden the terrorist nut jobs when they realize what girly-men American action heroes really are and how they sympathize with the terrorist's plight of having been abused by the mighty, evil empire. How shocking and disillusioning it was that not one young able bodied super stud from Hollyweird had the testicular fortitude to leap out of their make-up chair to take up arms and defend his country after the towers fell on 911. Hah! Not. It comes as no surprise whatsoever that these elitist cowards would sit home and give aid and comfort to our enemies. The best these negative Nancies could muster up was another well-choreographed, narcissistic performance showcasing their depth of feeling and compassion. The only problem is that it was difficult to discern if this genuine display of empathy was for the victims of 911 or the terrorists that perpetrated 911. When is the last time you heard one of these malicious movie stars denounce the fanatical Muslims and their actions?

What should we expect from a town that glorifies a no talent bimbo heiress whose only claim to fame is releasing a sex tape? Not only do these vacuous parasites get to ride the talk show circuit, get movie deals and videos, they get to be role models for our impressionable youth. Sadly, being famous for having sex on camera or being an alcoholic slash drug addict is not a strong enough message for the Academy of motion pictures and their screen actors guild cronies, they need to produce, promote, and reward a movie about a young teenage girl who gets pregnant, gives the baby away, and hasn't a care in the world. In Hollyweird children having sex and babies at any age is as acceptable as lemon grass smoothies and scientology.

So why does Hollywood want to destroy the

moral fabric of America? Is it because they'll feel better about their hedonistic lives if everyone else shares their perverted propensities? The truth is that actors, like politicians, thrive off the common working man. Hollywood needs the masses to be kept down. If the masses are down, then they can look up to their actor idols. It's a fine line when trying to keep a population in perpetual lower class. While Hollyweird needs to keep people down so they can only look up, they still need the masses to be able to afford a movie ticket and video rentals.

Elitism is the reason Hollywood's great philanderers and pundits blame the government for all the evil in country and for every poor person's lot in life. They are constantly yelping that our own problems have nothing to do with personal responsibility; they have everything to do with the government not giving us what we deserve. Hollywood's basic premise that our fate and happiness are controlled by the government is the same premise spewed by Jackson and Sharpton to the black community. When you're a hedonist, all your problems and issues are caused by someone or something else like the government.

Even though the truth is that these Hollyweird

pundits and their media partners are anti-patriotic, they love to quote our forefathers by claiming that dissent is the highest form of patriotism. This is a brilliant argument except for the facts that we are not in the middle of a revolution, are not being oppressed by a foreign or local government, and we now live in the greatest democracy that has ever existed. Arguing fervently against and even refusing to comply with policies like Jim Crow laws, illegal search and seizure, and greed based imminent domain cases are legitimate occurrences where dissent can be deemed patriotic. Rallying against the war because you have personal dislike for the commander in chief, giving comfort and aid to the enemy by reiterating their propaganda on film, and engaging in personal attacks and juvenile name calling can scarcely be construed as patriotism.

There are actually a few bright spots out there in the land of fruits and nuts. We have men like Bruce Willis, John Voight, and Kelsey Grammer who are conservatives or at least republicans. While these actors appear to be the minority, it is comforting to know there are a few of us out there fighting the good fight. Now, if we can just get Mister Voight to convert his daughter Angelina and his son-in-law Brad to conservatism, millions of the sheep-parrot hybrids would fall right inline. Could you imagine a Brangelina conservative movement? There would be riots in the Beverly Hills streets, total anarchy on every movie lot, and the left wing media would need to hold a solemn pagan funeral ritual for the death of their king and queen. The stunned looks of disbelief, the calls to have Mr. and Mrs. Jolie committed, and the accusations of the rightwing military's mind control device would be priceless.

Chapter 6
Activist Judges and Trial Lawyers

There are two simple solutions for dealing with activist judges at all levels of government. One solution is mandating that all judges be elected. Another part of the plan to halt the practice of making law from the bench is term limits. By having all judges answering to the people they are supposedly serving, they will be less likely to act as renegades and more likely to conform to the concerns of their constituents.

Establishing term limits for all judges at all levels with the exception of the Supreme Court, would make judges actually responsible to those they serve. If the judges are acting in accordance with our laws and constitution, then they like so many senators will have no problem getting themselves reelected. Obviously the Supreme Court is an extremely important body and competition among both parties is fierce to appoint a judge who shares their philosophy. It is easy to see how Republicans and Democrats alike will wince at the thought of actually making the appointment of Supreme Court Justices a fair competition by allowing the people to chose who represents one third of our federal government. Since every other branch of the federal government is kept in check by term limits, it is reasonable that the Supreme Court should not be immune from this process. However, our constitution states that Supreme Court Justices have lifetime appointments. Both conservatives and liberals must see the wisdom of this necessity before the balance of justice becomes permanently swayed to far in one direction.

Since the liberals abhor competition in any form, it is unlikely that they will ever go along with the ideas to level the playing field in the judicial arena. When the liberal left is getting the laws changed by activist judges to suit their whims and perversions, there is no reason for them to accept the terms of a fair election of judges by the people whom they were appointed to serve.

It is widely publicized that in the independent republic of Vermont, child rapists seem to be honorary members of the judges' fraternity. In San Francisco, judges routinely go against enacted laws and rule in whatever way their flamboyant fabulous selves see fit.

It makes no difference to them what referendum was passed by the people; these judicial dandies take it upon themselves to create precedents that allow themselves and their cult followers to circumvent the law and achieve the result they fairly and squarely lost in the house and senate.

When is the last time we heard a heated debate on torte reform in congress? With a nine per cent approval rating, it is fair to say congress has not been too busy debating much of anything. It is unclear if we should blame the greedy lawyers or the greedy people who hire them. When employees can sue for millions in a sexual harassment case because someone looked at them with one eyebrow raised, the system may have a flaw. When fast food patrons clumsily spill hot coffee in their laps and net a cool five million for that near death experience, we may have a problem with civil law.

Besides the countless number of frivolous law suits brought on by greedy citizens trying to bilk big business, there are far too many frivolous lawsuits crushing our medical system. Malpractice insurance is one main reason health care in this country is so expensive. If we put a stop to free health care for border criminals and stopped frivolous law suits against doctors and hospitals, health care in this country would be much more affordable. We have all been aware of this problem for years yet the problem remains. Of course, if a patient has the wrong leg amputated or has endured some other extreme negligence, they should be compensated. If patients merely suffer a bruise because they slipped, fell, or got bumped, then they should take their twenty dollar per tablet aspirin and shut up.

Let's be realistic, trial lawyers are not known for their high character, ethics, or aspirations. Lawyers are known for their high fees and ability to manipulate facts. What other profession can have the audacity to bill for pense charges. Only lawyers can say that they spent two hours thinking about your case and charge you four hundred dollars. If everyone got paid whenever they thought about their job, even an average burger flipper could retire at age thirty.

Thank God lawyers aren't running the country. Right Mister and Misses Clinton, Obama, Edwards half of congress, and the Supreme Court? It is no coincidence that so many politicians are lawyers. Being able to speak eloquently for twenty minutes about an issue and still not really say anything is a skill taught at the most prestigious law schools in the country. Perhaps instead of having lawyer as a resume qualification for politicians, we should make being a trial lawyer a disqualifier. Having no lawyers in government would make it much easier for us to know who is telling the truth and who is really not answering the questions.

If lawyers were seated at the top of our government hierarchy, we could end up with a President who sends the message by example to all of our youth above the age of reason that it is ok to commit adultery with fat ugly women and then lie about it under oath. Oh wait, we did that already. Well, at least Clinton's wife wasn't battling cancer at the time. That would have been really low. Oh wait, we did that too.

Is it a coincidence that Edwards and Clinton are both lawyers and both cheaters? At least Edwards had the sense not to perjure himself in the process of cheating on his cancer stricken wife with some bimbo who admittedly believes he is he next Gandhi. It is frightening how these liberal lunatics are actually taken in by the lawyer double speak. What these lawyer politician groupies fail to see is that their heroes are no different then them. Both Clinton and Edwards were super smooth talkers and presented themselves as saviors to the down trodden. All the while these deliverers of the lower class were talking out of one side of their legal trained mouths; they were seeking nothing more than to satisfy their thirst for power, world-wide recognition, and sex with mindless bimbos.

Chapter 7
Why Liberals Hate President Bush

To put it simply, liberals hate bush because he is an evangelical and they believe he stole the election. As discussed in chapter three, liberals detest God and anyone whose character and wisdom is based on a secure foundation of faith in God. Not only does President Bush rely on his faith to guide his decisions, he is not ashamed to let the world know that he derives his strength and comfort from his Christian beliefs.

To liberals, President Bush embodies the exact opposite of what their leader should be. He is calm, strong, and unwavering in his convictions. He does not bend to polls, public opinion, or the constant whining from the celebutants. President Bush inherited numerous crises from his predecessor Clinton and is still dealing with the clean up.

Thanks to Clinton's brilliant plan to decimate our military and intelligence services, we were treated to 9/11. If Clinton were as wise as the Scientologists would have you believe, he would have neutered himself instead of our military and intelligence services thus avoiding a tarnished legacy as well as 9/11. In the naïve twisted minds of liberals like Clinton and his followers, America is evil and the military serves as the vehicle to carry out our evil ambitions. Also, liberals believe that if we all just smoke pot, hold hands, and sing Kumbaya all the world will love us and we will never need to defend ourselves.

President Bush was also rewarded with an atomic threat from North Korea and an end to the Internet bubble thanks to the almighty man who preferred flesh humidors. Nevertheless, the liberals condemn the Bush policies dealing with North Korea all the while forgetting that Clinton gave them nuclear technology as part of an extortion payoff. Similarly, the liberal pundits wax romantically at how the great Clinton created an economic utopia and made life wonderful for all. Never mind the fact that the prosperity Clinton created only existed on paper and collapsed right when he left office. The truth is that every good thing Clinton did in office was brought about by Newt Gingrich's contract with America.

Thank God President Bush was elected in 2000. Who amongst us with any hint of a brain was not thankful and relieved that the President during 9/11 was George W. Bush? While the liberals believe that if we caught Bin Laden everything would be as wonderful the bridge of the Star Trek enterprise, Bush knew that the war against terror would be a long-term, world wide conflict requiring great resources serving many arenas. Can you imagine if Al Gore was President during 9/11? We would be fighting battles in hybrid jets while dropping bombs made of biodegradable cardboard filled with corn.

Like it or not we are at war with radical Islam. While liberals prefer to have a Jimmy Carter in the commander in chief seat and condemn Bush as a hawkish cowboy, real men are grateful we have a cowboy with Texas values in charge of our armed forces.

Throughout President Bush's aggressive fight against terror, he has been handicapped every step of the way by liberal whiners. Liberals are petrified by the patriot act. The thought of someone knowing what they buy or read is so invasive and shameful; they would rather die in another terrorist attack than have someone realize they are nerdy perverts. Look, if you're a forty year old male virgin living with your mother and are embarrassed that the government is going to find out that you visit the library weekly to read Danielle Steele novels, perhaps you should just go to the used book store and pay cash. Likewise if you're a liberal worried about the government becoming aware that you are spending so much time surfing the Internet to satisfy your hedonistic perversions, that stepping out into the sun actually causes you pain, you might want to remove your tinfoil hat and cut down web surfing just a tad. The government does not care what you read, buy, say on the phone, or see on the Internet unless it is against the law or is a threat to national security. The amount of arrogance required by these ACLU loving rejects to believe that the government is watching their every move is astonishing and borderline psychotic.

Another reason liberals hate Bush may have to do with the women in his life. Let's compare Laura Bush and Hillary Clinton as first lady. First of all, unlike Hillary, Laura Bush is a lady. She conducts herself with grace, class, charm, and wisdom at all times and will be remembered as a true American Patriot and champion of many charitable causes, while remembrances of Hillary seeking the presidency will always remind some of Gollum trying to get his ring back.

Contrast Laura Bush's persona to that of Hillary. Hillary will always be known as a corrupt lawyer who stopped at nothing to grasp the reigns of power including overlooking the constant infidelity of her likewise corrupt lawyer husband. It has been hinted at by some that Hillary never recovered from the fact that she was born without a penis and she will do whatever it takes short of surgery to hide that fact.

While Laura Bush was learning to educate our youth, Hillary was becoming a professional liar. While Mrs. Bush spent her time as first lady combating disease and poverty world-wide, Hillary spent her time as first lady failing to socialize medicine and plotting her rise to power in New York. Now ask yourself, who is the greater American? Which would you chose as a role model for your daughter?

While Bill Clinton had Madeline Albright as secretary of state, Bush had Condoleezza Rice. While Albright was busy giving nuclear technology to North Korea and assuring the world that the United States was as powerful as a de-clawed kitten, Condoleezza was acquiring wisdom. It's hilarious that liberals would have you believe that conservatives are all bigots, all the while the highest ranking black person ever to serve in a

Presidential cabinet was appointed by Bush.

Liberals would argue that Bush appointed Rice so that he would appear not to be prejudiced. There is no way on earth that such an important position in the United States could ever have been given to someone for show and not for substance and there is no way an incompetent person could last as secretary of state for eight years in these times of global turmoil. The fact is that Bush saw beyond race and gender and chose the best person for the job.

Another reason liberals abhor Bush is that he allows big business to actually keep some of their profits. In the demented liberal mind, any entity or individual that manages to achieve a certain amount of wealth is deemed evil. President Bush had the sense to cut taxes on big business and capital gains. Bush like Reagan realized that businesses create jobs and the more success a business enjoys, the more its employees will benefit. Also, the more prosperity is proliferated through the strata of society, the more revenue the government obtains.

Despite the fact that Bush was handed an illusion of a healthy economy, a decimated military and intelligence force, and 9/11, he managed to keep the economy growing. Liberals argue that the war is a waste of our (Republicans) hard earned treasure and the treasure would be better spent subsidizing socialist projects. What Obama calls "economic justice" is liberal code for Socialism. The truth is that if we do not secure our nation from threats abroad, none of this will matter because our economy will soon be discussed in Arabic.

President George W. Bush will be remembered as the man who realized that free people are happy, content people. Bush will be remembered as the president who had the vision and strength to employ freedom as our greatest weapon against terror. By giving the Iraqi and Afghanis the responsibility and freedom to run their own lives, President Bush has given them something to fight for and protect. Our new democratic allies will fight for what they believe in not because a dictator says they must, but because they now realize that they are in charge of their own communities, families, and destinies.

President George W. Bush will also be remembered as a man who stood firm for what he believed. A man who knew what was best for the United States and the rest of the free world and as a man who did whatever he could to make sure that no one or no group was allowed to bring harm to us or our way of life. All the while the chic socialists in Hollywierd and Europe are besmirching the great man, they are basking in the freedom and security that he has fought so hard to preserve and protect.

Chapter 8
The Far-left's Tolerance of Radical Islam

When the far-left speaks of religious intolerance, they never speak of fanatical Islam. What the liberals object to is family values and the ideals which help to foster clean living. You never hear a liberal chastising Muslims for their gross mistreatment of women, Jews, or any infidel that does not agree with their paranoid philosophies. The fact is that Islam is the most intolerant religion on the planet. Covering a painting of the Madonna with feces is perfectly acceptable to the far-left but publishing a cartoon satirizing Allah is grounds for war.

Despite 9/11 and the murder of thousands of innocent civilians using airplanes, Muslims and the lefties are amazed that security forces have the audacity to profile Muslims at the airport. If all the highjackers were eighty year old white women, then we would all be nervous when we saw a champion bridge playing team boarding our flight.

These fanatical Muslim men are so anxious regarding their women that they are driven to a homicidal rage at the thought of another man catching a glimpse of their beloved's ankle. Ahmed, relax, they make pills for that now which will allow you to keep her satisfied. Where are the militant feminists in the fight against this injustice? They are busy trying to turn little boys into little girls. The far-left feminists have no problem with fanatical Muslims castrating little girls or executing women for committing adultery just as long as in this country Julie can play on the boy's high school football team.

The ultimate absurdity of these tuned-out turban wearers was the call to murder a kindergarten teacher who had the insane idea to name a class teddy bear Allah. Can you imagine the gall of this woman? If Christians behaved this was we would have a genocide limited to every Hispanic named Jesus. It is not clear whether the naming of a teddy bear or the publishing of a cartoon are really that offensive to Muslims or if the Muslims are really just seeking out any excuse to exercise their rage and hatred of the west. In order to test whether Muslims are really that sensitive, henceforth let it be known that the author of this book has decried that the bottom of his left shoe will forever after be known as Allah 1 and the bottom of his right shoe will be forever known as Allah 2. Now if the author of this book is assassinated in a drive-by involving a camel or is named to the Al Qaeda top ten most wanted list, we can conclude that these fanatical Muslims are just ultra-sensitive souls or maybe just a little too high strung.

Despite the ridiculousness of these fanatical Muslim beliefs and actions, the far-left would have you believe that their hatred and intolerance of the west is our own government's fault. If we look at this closer, it may be fairer to say that the far-left is responsible. Which group in the United States promotes those values which Muslims hate the most? Which group promotes promiscuity, sloth, and weakness? You guessed it, the far left. Now half of the far-left will tell you that Bush's foreign policy is why they hate us. If Bush wasn't in Saudi Arabia then 9/11 would have never happened. The other half will tell you that Bush masterminded 9/11. The truth is that no matter what we say or do fanatical Islam is hell bent on our destruction and the sooner the far-left appeasement movement realizes this, the quicker we can crush fanatical Islam and its progenitors.

The lack of the far-left's outcry and action against militant Islam is no different than actively supporting them. By blaming the United States for 3000 dead in September 2001 and keeping silent regarding the brutality of the fanatical regimes, the far-left nut jobs are supporting the very people who would kill us all. These are the same cowards who went berserk over the mistreatment of prisoners at Abu Ghraib. Oh my goodness some unlucky murdering rapist got caught, was stripped naked, and had his weenie laughed at by a woman with a gun. Oh the humanity. Meanwhile, there are thousands of people in San Francisco who pay good money for an experience like that. While these forsaken, abused, delicate killers' are suffering their deserved humiliation, their counterparts are cutting the heads off of innocent reporters. Oddly enough there was no outrage from the far-left over the decapitations, only outrage regarding the mistreatment of those who would kill them where they stand.

A swift death is too good for those seeking seventy-two virgins in the afterlife. Hey Mohamed, no one said they will stay virgins. What will you do with the rest of eternity after you used them all up? How blatant is the irony and hypocrisy that the highest ambition of these religious morons is sex with seventy-two different women in the after life, while here on earth their wives are so socially repressed that they are not even allowed to be seen in public and dating more than one man results in an honor killing.

Where are the far-left protests regarding the murder of Jews in Israel? There is none. In the liberal left thinking, Israel should just placate the Muslims and give them more land. They tried it – it didn't work. The truth is as much as they hate the west, fanatical Muslims hate Jews even more. No matter what concessions Israel makes, Iran and its kin will never be satisfied until Israel is annihilated. Israel and the Jewish people have suffered enough. While Israel has a tiny spot of land to call home, Muslims have the entire Middle East to wallow in their ignorance. That's enough. That's all they get. Israel is Israel and needs to stay way it is. Israel needs to make no more concessions or engage in anymore negotiations they have given up more than they should and have suffered more than is imaginable at the hands of their intolerant, zealous neighbors.

One would think that the fact that the far-left worships Darwin and his laws of natural selection and survival of the fittest as an alternative to God would give us the green light to trounce our enemies with great efficiency. If we humans are merely a highly evolved species of ape, then the queasy liberals should have no grievance with the United States ruthlessly eliminating our enemies. Darwinism only appeals to liberals insofar as it can be translated into an argument against there being a God. Muslims killing Americans means nothing to the far-left so long as the polar bears don't have to swim to far to catch a seal.

The United States has does not thrive on resentments or vindictiveness but has an enormous capacity to forgive. While most people in the United States have forgiven Japan and Germany for their actions in the past, few have forgiven or are likely to forgive the radical factions of Islam for their horrific acts of terrorism. The reasoning behind this discrepancy is simple, Japan and Germany saw the light, repented, and became great nations of free and enlightened people. On the other hand, many Muslim nations are unrepentant, still in the dark, and are steadfastly continuing their plans to destroy our people and way of life. Until Muslims stop teaching their babies to hate and kill the Jewish people and westerners, there can be no peace.

Conclusion

Whether it's mass delusion, group hypnosis, or a genetic anomaly, the far-left have a psychosis all their own. It can be argued that the leftist loons are in touch with reality and therefore not actually psychotic. After all, they know exactly what they are doing and engage in shrewd tactics to achieve their objectives. The fact that the far-left who want to sabotage our security, unconditionally open our borders, expunge God from all thought, erase the family unit, and allow all forms of debauchery to become mainstream, are by far the minority. The reality of these hedonistic groups is not the reality of the vast majority of the United States and therefore geocentrically psychotic.

The fact that these groups think that the government can pay for all their needs and pleasures while they do nothing but bash the government and troops that protect them certainly hints at a break with reality. If everyone gets food stamps, free health care, free housing, and social security disability because they are depressed, the United States will fall like the Soviet Union.

We cannot lose the war in Iraq. We cannot let the liberals pretend to support the troops and bite their lips every time there is good news from Iraq. The liberals seemed to have learned their lesson from Vietnam about treating our soldiers with respect, but they forgot the lesson about losing. In San Francisco they actually had the nerve to try and ban military recruiters from operating in the city. If San Francisco is ever attacked or invaded by terrorists, it would not be surprising if the military took their sweet old time coming to the rescue. If we actually came together as a country like we did in World War II and ignored the ignorant that cannot see the big picture, the war in Iraq would have been over years ago and they would already have an Iraqi Disneyland.

Even though the extreme far left is presently in the great minority, the far left is growing at an alarming pace. With pregnant children being celebrated, gay marriage taking place, entire cities being built just to engage in sex and gambling, and God's place in our culture being actively threatened, America is in grave danger of becoming a third world nation. Without strong family values, strong military and intelligence services, and vital competition in the market place, we will be at the mercy of those who would do us harm.

Many who read this book will see it as an affirmation that right-wing conservatives are all xenophobic, greedy businessmen, and war-mongers. The truth is that conservatives do not see people of color, conservatives see people who work hard, believe in self reliance, believe in traditional values, and those who do not. Conservatives do not hold ill will to people of any race, creed, or gender; conservatives are disturbed by those who actively seek to destroy our way of life by sponging off the government and weakening our security. We must prevent these hedonistic, liberals from working hard to leave our country vulnerable, eliminating God from society, and obliterating the family unit.